I0484242

THE LITTLE BOND eBOOKLET
Must-knows about your bond portfolio

By Marilyn Cohen and Chris Malburg

Also by Marilyn Cohen and Chris Malburg

Bonds Now!
Surviving the Bond Bear Market:
Bondland's Nuclear Winter
The Bond Bible

* * * *

THE LITTLE BOND eBOOKLET

By Marilyn Cohen and Chris Malburg

Library of Congress Cataloging-in-Publication Data
Cohen, Marilyn and Malburg, Chris
The Little Bond eBooklet / Marilyn Cohen Chris Malburg
Library of Congress Control Number: Pending
ISBN 978-1511675352

1. Bonds. 2. Interest rates. 3. Yield 4. Marilyn Cohen 5. Chris Malburg. 6. Municipal bonds 7. Corporate bonds 8. Bond yield

Table of Contents

Welcome to The Little Bond *e*Booklet

There once was a time when investors could buy bonds—municipals or corporates, take your pick—set it and forget it. The chances were slim that the floor would fall out from under the bond's price. Bondholders were secure in the knowledge that their investment would keep on paying its coupon year after year. Life was good.

But this financial Camelot came to an end during 2008. America—along with the rest of the world—suffered one of the worst financial meltdowns in history. The entire financial community was involved in some way. Most pointed the finger at the home mortgage lenders. They loaned money to unqualified homebuyers at rates and terms that proved suicidal. Then they securitized these loans and sold them to institutional investors. These unqualified borrowers eventually failed to meet their mortgage obligations. Then the entire house of cards collapsed.

With this collapse, the financial landscape changed forever. New regulations—many say overly restrictive regulations—now control the banking and financial services industry. Couple that with the fiscal irresponsibility of many municipal bond issuers—states, counties, cities, and districts—and once again fixed income investors face a dilemma.

With the increased federal tax rates that began in 2014, high net worth investors need securities in their portfolios that stave off at least some of this tax bite. The urgency is even greater for those living in states where state income tax is a way of life. For these investors, there has never been a more compelling time to own municipal bonds.

The laws of economics are hard at work here. Demand for munis grows, as supply stays flat or falls. Bond investors must understand these dynamics and act in their own best interests.

The Little Bond eBooklet is a quick and simple guide for municipal and corporate bond investors. We hit only the highlights of individual bonds. Our intent is to identify the biggest issues facing bond investors. Since this is a short booklet, we won't discuss how the bond market problems came about. That's history. Instead, we'll tell you what actions you need to take now to protect your investment portfolio. We explain the problem, illustrate the damage it can do to your portfolio and offer up some solutions to protect yourself. All in the space of this short booklet. There's no time to waste. Let's begin.

* * *

Chapter 1: Municipal Bonds
Weak municipal bond issuers

The problem
Economic influences have significantly weakened many municipal bond issuers. Some problems are self-inflicted by politically motivated, incompetent, and/or corrupt government officials. Among the biggest problems are unfunded pension liabilities. The most prominent of these weakened issuers are Puerto Rico, Chicago, New Jersey, and Illinois. Whatever the cause, the problems these issuers face must not become yours.

The damage: Unbridled ambition
Suddenly fiscally weakened issuers are subject to credit rating downgrades by the rating agencies—Moody's, Standard & Poors, and Fitch. Bonds that abruptly get downgraded may not only plummet in value, but are difficult to sell because the universe of municipal junk bonds is small.

However, many investors are skeptical of the very rating agencies passing judgment on these bond issues. This problem has many facets. First is the history of these rating agencies. During the 2008 market collapse, many of the bonds that tanked carried stellar ratings. Why? One reason has to do with a lack of independence. The very issuers the agencies are rating pay their fee. Before the 2008 market implosion some said this financial connection sometimes influenced the final rating.

Another independence issue goes to the ambition of the analysts doing the ratings.

Since 2008, 300 analysts have left rating agencies for jobs at Wall Street banks. A case in point involves Michelle Choi, an analyst for Moody's. She rated bonds issued by Evansham Township, New Jersey. The bond's underwriters, Morgan Stanley, offered her a job. The timing looks questionable. Even though there may have been nothing wrong here, it *has the appearance* that Ms. Choi may not have been independent of her analysis.

The damage: Downgraded ratings

Many of the institutional money managers have a prescribed bond rating their holdings cannot fall below. If a rating downgrade occurs that puts an issue below that threshold, they must sell. Immediately. Imagine all those institutional sellers with the same mandate selling hundreds of millions of the same bonds because the rating agencies have signaled a risk. Now imagine watching your own holdings of this same issue tumbling in value *and you're powerless to stop it because you cannot find a buyer.*

News of the day and the underlying economic shifts can and do affect bond ratings. A current example occurred in California's oil patch. As oil prices have plummeted, so have some of the revenues from municipalities where the oil is produced. Kern County, located in California's Central Valley, is among the largest oil producers in the continental US. The County's board of supervisors has declared a fiscal emergency as oil prices decline. As a result of this revenue downturn, Standard & Poors revised its outlook for Kern County from stable to negative on its certificates of participation and its pension obligation bonds (neither of which we advise owning anyway). Because of Kern's reliance on oil-associated revenues it will suffer a $27 million budget shortfall in fiscal 2016. With this downgrade, the underlying bonds are certainly affected.

The Damage: Puerto Rico

At Envision Capital in the past, we had some clients who held Puerto Rico bonds. Not now. There are many individual investors around the country with these bonds. So, let's take the case of Puerto Rico. S&P has finally downgraded Puerto Rico. These bonds are pure junk.

When a municipality or municipal agency asks for more time to pay their debts—as has the Puerto Rico Power Agency, Prepa—there's a problem. Then Prepa begins discussions for a debt restructuring. To us, this clearly signals a potential default. The old saying, *if it walks like a duck...* comes to mind.

Puerto Rico has a population of less than 4 million people. Yet it has $70 billion in debt and $33 billion in underfunded pensions. Only 25 percent of its people have jobs and of those, 27 percent work for the government. Finally, employment in the private sector is a measly 647,000 people.

This tiny island nation cannot possibly honor its $70 billion debt.

S&P is the first rating agency to downgrade Puerto Rico's credit worthiness. S&P moved its rating of Puerto Rico's General Obligation bonds from BBB- to BB+ —a move that booted Puerto Rico out of the investment grade category and into junk bond territory. They also saw fit to downgrade the Commonwealth's appropriation secured debt and Puerto Rico's Employee Retirement System debt to BB. Finally, in their press release, S&P found it necessary to reiterate that their ratings related to Puerto Rico remain on CreditWatch with negative implications. Puerto Rico's bond yields were already distressed way before S&P saw fit to tell the truth.

What took the rating agencies so long to act on something the Street has seen for some time? Here's our theory: S&P might have reasoned that downgrading a significant holding could cause a negative impact in the overall debt market. There's the law of unintended consequences. Who wants a role—any role—in starting an avalanche of bond market problems? So they waited. And waited. Finally, the handwriting was on the wall and S&P had to act.

Conclusion: If you own any Puerto Rico municipal bonds—other than those that are prerefunded—sell them. Take the hit and move on. Defaults and restructuring are looming.

The damage: Bankruptcy

Bankruptcy is now a solution sought by weakened issuers. Detroit and Stockton, CA have already gone through bankruptcy. Chicago, and Atlantic City look like good candidates for bankruptcy or at least restructuring. Understand that states by law cannot declare bankruptcy. However, cities can and do, under Chapter 9 of the Bankruptcy statutes. Holders of bonds whose issuers are in bankruptcy or restructure will lose some of their principal.

Case in point: Atlantic City

Here's an example of the type of reasoning we professionals go through when assessing a problem credit. Let's say you're considering an investment in Atlantic City bonds. We know it has twelve casinos. At one time they comprised 70% of the city's property tax base. But now four of those casinos are closed. Not good news. And competition for gambling dollars is fierce. Atlantic City's casino revenue in 2006 was $5.2 billion. By 2014 it had fallen to just $2.5 billion. The city is deeply in debt.

According to Bloomberg News, Atlantic City has borrowed $345 million since 2010. This money went to plug municipal deficits and tax appeals. Debt service—the money needed to repay principal and keep current on interest—now accounts for a whopping 15% of Atlantic City's budget. All this has caused Moody's to downgrade Atlantic City's general obligation debt from Ba1 to

Caa1—a high risk of default over the next five years.

New Jersey Governor Christie issued an executive order and assembled an emergency management and turnaround team. But, guess whom he named as the special consultant advising on this undertaking? Kevyn Orr. Yes, the very same Kevyn Orr who advised on putting Detroit into bankruptcy. Orr is the guy who helped make the decision to screw Detroit's bondholders in favor of the pensions. Those holding Detroit bonds came away with pennies on the dollar while the pensions faired much better, taking just a 20% haircut in benefits. There's a saying that comes to mind: *When all you have is a hammer, everything looks like a nail.* Should Orr's advice result in Atlantic City filing for bankruptcy, bondholders will likely get the short end of the stick again.

Atlantic City's cash is dwindling. Pension payment obligations are piling up. Things look grim for Atlantic City. Price and yield on their bonds tell the story: Atlantic City New Jersey General Obligation bonds maturing Feb. 2020 yield 5.70%. This is a bad omen. Our conclusion: Stay away from Atlantic City bonds.

The damage: Political expediency
Local politics too often influence far-reaching decisions important to municipal bonds. Examples come from Pennsylvania, Kansas, and Kentucky. All three states are drowning in unfunded pension liabilities. In

their unending effort to get themselves reelected the politicos-turned-financial geniuses in Kentucky are planning on borrowing $3.3 billion using a pension bond issue. They plan on investing this money and earning a greater appreciation rate than the interest cost on the bonds. Sounds like a good idea. Until, you remember that the equity markets have hit all-time highs. How much higher do these savants think it will go before it retreats? Further, there's a rate for every risk—meaning they're increasing the risk of their investment portfolios.

A decade ago Illinois and New Jersey tried the same thing. The market went against them. Their pension payments fell behind. Now they're in even worse shape than if they had never issued the pension bonds in the first place.

Kansas Governor, Sam Brownback, apparently thinks the stock market is on a long-term climb too. He's proposing a $1.5 billion pension bond issue with the same goal of arbitraging the portfolio appreciation against the interest cost on the bonds. These pension bond issues generally go against professional wisdom and advice. The Government Finance Officers Association recommends against it. Blackrock, a manager overseeing $116 billion in state and local debt, is against it too. So are we at Envision Capital Management, Inc.

Lastly, this strategy might well succeed for a year or two. But pension bonds are much longer-term instruments. That means they must beat the market more often than not during the course of the bond's term.

Unlikely, we think. Few but the politicians like pension bonds. They are a red flag that something is drastically wrong with the way the entity is budgeting and allocating its money. Stay away from pension bonds.

The solution
The best solution is vigilance. Watch every bond in your portfolio. Conduct your review frequently. Stay in touch with the news on your issuers. Negative news often signals more to come.

State policy on market access
It's okay to look at a bond issued by a municipality that appears shaky. However, you need to look first at the state's policy related to capital market access by its municipalities. States like Rhode Island and New York protect capital market access for their municipalities. When Central Falls, RI went bankrupt, the bonds remained unimpaired. The state stepped in and made everyone whole. Good for the bondholders, but not so good for labor, pensions and other post-employment beneficiaries who suffered severe cuts in their benefits.

On the other hand, states like California and Michigan refuse to protect their municipalities from the effects of filing for bankruptcy. When Detroit settled with their creditors, the emergency manager—with the state's approval—disregarded the bond covenants and gave the pensions (comprised of voters) only a small haircut on their benefits. Bondholders (not voters), on the other hand, lost hundreds of millions.

Always examine the issuing state's policy and history of supporting its problem cities. States with unfunded pension liabilities, spending that outstrip income and that have no commitment to protecting capital market access pose a greater risk than others. Likewise, those states with a history of pandering to a voter constituency.

Security features
Many bonds have specific security features that enhance their safety for investors. Certainly, you'll pay for these in terms of a lower yield. There are bonds secured by special revenues or statutory liens. Often there are special purpose authorities created specifically to provide bankruptcy protection. The Municipal Assistance Corporation was one such entity.

On the opposite side are Certificates of Participation, Lease Revenue Bonds, and bonds issued to build entertainment venues, sports arenas, and golf courses. We almost always avoid such bonds. They carry a risk to our investors and have no place in their portfolios. The same goes for unsecured pension obligation bonds. Treatment of these bonds in the event of a financial catastrophe by the issuer will become a matter of public policy and politics rather than the rule of law governing the bond indenture.

Information sources
Among the best information sources is the Website, www.emma.msrb.org sponsored

by the Municipal Securities Rulemaking Board. Should they issue notification of a Material Event on a bond you own, pay attention—it is seldom good news.

The final solution is to sell when you need to—don't wait. Here at Envision Capital, our motto is, *when in doubt, get out*. The few dollars in income you may lose by selling too soon is nothing compared to the catastrophic loss of principal should your issuer fail to honor its obligations.

* * *

Chapter 2: Failure To Issue Financial Statements

The SEC requires all entities issuing public equity or debt to provide financial statements at least annually. That's not usually a problem for most issuers of public debt. After all, it demonstrates a level of transparency to the public debt investors. That's a good thing. But there are some municipalities that fail to issue their financial statements when required.

When a municipality fails to disclose financial results, investors are flying blind. They have no idea of certain specific data points every bond investor needs to know:

1. Cash reserves
2. Current income and projected income
3. Spending and projected spending
4. The amount by which income exceeds (or falls short) of spending
5. Unfunded liabilities such as pensions and accounts payable

These are very simple financial indicators of an issuer's stability. Failure to provide them to investors draws in the complaint, *we don't know what we don't know.*

A publicly traded company that fails to report its financial information quarterly will quickly see its share price plummet and may even be delisted by its stock exchange. That's punishment well deserved.

Disclosure requirements for debt-issuing municipalities include annual financial statements. That sets the bar pretty low. Publicly traded companies must issue their financials quarterly—only a slightly higher bar. Yet some municipalities either cannot or will not provide their financial statements. This failure shows investors no love or respect and very little financial competency. The next question a skeptical bond investor should ask is, *what else are you hiding?*

Damage: Failure to disclose financial information

When a new client comes to us with municipal holdings that have no current financials, we sell them immediately. It surely doesn't mean the bond issuers will soon declare bankruptcy. Nor is it an indicator of fraud. But it does show a lack of abiding by the municipal bond rules and regulations. A management demonstrating this lack of regard and transparency for the bondholder is not a management in which anyone should invest, least of all our clients.

Here's what happens when a well-known municipality—Harrisburg, PA—thumbed their nose at the law.

Around mid-May of 2013, the SEC charged Harrisburg with securities fraud. That's a serious allegation. It stems from misrepresenting their financial condition as being better than it was while it further deteriorated.

The City of Harrisburg failed to disclose required financial information to the

Municipal Securities Rulemaking Board's (MSRB) Electronic Municipal Market Access (EMMA) system. Actually, they filed their 2009 financial statements two years late. Their 2010 financials were just a year late.

This placed investors in the position of seeking alternative sources for the financial information needed to make their investment decisions. They found it. Harrisburg's mayor compounded the city's problem by deliberately making false public statements about its credit rating, financial condition, and timeliness of debt payments. Mr. Mayor assured the public that any financial issues "can be resolved". This proved untrue.

One would think that a small municipality failing to file its financial statements is one thing. But what happens when an entire *state* fails to file? New Mexico has a problem filing its financial statements in a timely manner. New Mexico's Comprehensive Audited Financial Report was not audited at all for 2012. Its 2014 report was late and its auditors could not give it an unqualified (so-called clean) opinion. Of the issues preventing its auditors from opining on New Mexico's financials were:

- Inadequate controls

- Improper consolidation of all the entities comprising the state's financials

- Non disclosure of all events occurring after the audit cutoff date

- Non disclosure of potential contingencies

However, despite these failings, Standard & Poor's rated New Mexico as AA+. Still, they did cut their outlook from stable to negative.

Damage: Manipulating financial results

Cooking the books is the act of making financial statements appear to show something other than the truth—usually overstating results. It is a financial crime. Yet, in the case of cooking the books, the financial statements were indeed filed. They were just deliberately inflated. Until recently municipal bond regulators were reluctant to level punitive actions against municipalities for diverting funds and cooking the books to cover up the act. The regulator's history of just giving a rap on the knuckles only punished investors rather than those who committed the act of fraud.

Harvey, IL offers an example of such non-punishment. The Court found Harvey's comptroller, Joe Letke, to have diverted millions in funds from a recent bond issue to other projects and into his own pocket. His punishment is what seemed outrageous. Letke paid a fine equivalent to a fraction of what he stole. The Court at least had the good sense to bar him from ever participating in a municipal bond offering again. As for the city of Harvey, they were allowed to neither admit nor deny any wrongdoing. They also promised to stop violating federal securities law and to hire a new consultant rather than Joe Letke in the future.

Some may dismiss such acts by small cities as not being representative of the way states conduct their business. Not so. Recently the SEC slapped charges of civil fraud on the State of Illinois. Apparently the state failed to provide adequate disclosure of its hugely underfunded public pensions.

Not to be left out, the State of New Jersey was charged with fraudulent bond offerings. The court order states that New Jersey has a, "significant disregard…for the principles of fair and accurate disclosure."

Is it any wonder that our policy at Envision Capital is to sell any bond whose issuer fails to timely file its financial statements? We add to this the caveat that the filed statements must be correct as attested to by a reputable certified public accounting firm.

Damage: Credit rating downgrades
Until only recently there was little push back to those municipalities that failed to disclose their financial statements. Then Moody's rating service finally grew a pair. They yanked their ratings on 25 municipalities that failed to issue financial statements. Now these bonds float out there in the unrated ether. Few institutional investors are allowed to hold unrated bonds. They sold these issues as soon as they became unrated. If a large number of bonds suddenly flooded the market, prices for these bonds would gyrate.

We view this occurrence as avoidable. Had these bondholders done their homework, they would have noticed that their bond issuers failed to issue financial statements. They could have done something—like sell them.

We agree with Moody's. These issuers don't deserve to be rated. Most do-it-yourself investors we know don't buy unrated munis. Only junk municipal bond funds, speculators, and a few risk takers who know what they're doing inhabit the unrated sector.

Damage: The list of nondisclosures
Here's the list of New York issuers that Moody's will no longer rate:

Village of Airmont
Lake Luzerne
Stone Ridge Fire Dist.
Woodbury
Town of Bolton
Lansing
Schodack
Wawayanda
Town of Boston
North Dansville
Schaghticoke
Watertown
Town of Busti
North Greenbush
Royalton
Volney
Cicero
Town of Greenport
City of Johnstown
Virgil
Dickinson

City of Gloversville
Fort Ann
Esopus
Erwin

If you own any bonds issued by these municipalities or districts, sell them.

Damage: Failure to comply with the Official Statement

The most important document to a new municipal bond offering is the Official Statement. Consider this your bible. It shows in excruciating detail how and where the bond proceeds will be spent once the bonds are issued. Senior executives of the bond issuer must sign off on the Official Statement. Their signature(s) attest to the validity of the financial statements, sources and uses of funds, debt service coverage calculations, and cash reserves. Any wrong information appearing in the Official Statement is the fault of those signatories. And they will be held responsible.

Should issuers lie about the facts or fail to execute what the Official Statement says they will—as in the case of Harvey, IL, the state of Illinois, and the state of New Jersey—the entire bond issue may crater into a morass of incredulity. That's when the regulators must step in—with an Abrams tank rather than their usual fly swatter that does little in the way of deterring others.

The regulators are there to protect the retail investors. There should be significant punishment for those who break securities laws.

When determining if a new issue belongs in your bond portfolio, ask these questions as you study the Official Statement:

1. Did past bond issues comply with the promises made?

2. Was there litigation due to non-compliance?

3. Did the issuer actually disburse the money the way the Official Statement said they would?

Even one instance of noncompliance with the Official Statement is one too many. As with the cockroach theory—there's never just one.

Damage: An awakened SEC
The SEC has been known for having more flash than brass. That's a polite way of saying they did less than they could have to enforce the United States securities laws. Their enforcement personnel are smart, upwardly mobile young people. Often the SEC is merely a short stepping-stone to Wall Street where the real money is made. As a result, investigations and enforcement actions were often slow or nonexistent. After all, who wants to upset a prospective employer who will make them millionaires?

Now, things are changing over at the SEC. The municipal securities enforcement division seems to have found religion. A recent example came when the SEC leveled charges of security fraud against the city of Miami and its former budget director. The

Commission alleges the former budget director transferred funds among various city accounts to hide deficits in the city's general fund. He did this in order to make the city's fiscal stability appear better than it was to both investors and bond-rating agencies. The charges also flow to the city's alleged misrepresentations in its 2007 and 2008 Comprehensive Annual Financial Report (which appears in the Official Statement) and in communications with rating agencies in 2009.

Still, with the SEC's history of complacency, we urge all municipal bond investors to exercise the utmost diligence in making their buy/sell decisions.

Solution

When financial statements are issued, review them. Check them for the simple indicators listed earlier—cash reserves, income greater than expenditures, and unfunded liabilities.

If they miss issuing their financial statements, find out why. Even though we haven't heard a plausible excuse yet, there could be a first time. Watch for drops in revenue or increases in spending. If projected spending exceeds anticipated revenues, find out how the shortfall will be extinguished. Too often, by glomming on more bond debt. Decide for yourself if the issuer can handle the additional debt service without a ratings downgrade.

Always scan your monthly statements and your online alerts for investment grade municipal bonds that were downgraded and have sunk into the junk pile. Keep tabs on your muni holdings and their financials at the MSRB website, www.emma.msrb.org .

So what municipal bonds should investors be buying? The next section deals with State Intercept Bonds and other safety nets.

* * *

Chapter 3: Not All Safety Nets Are Created Equal

Most fixed income investors buy their bonds based on the credit worthiness of the bond issuer. That's what we do at Envision Capital. Good investors analyze the issuer's financial statements, credit history, and compliance with the law. They watch the headlines for any problems—minor or major. They watch the revenue and expenses, being sure that revenues exceed expenses. When it comes time to sell, they don't hesitate.

General Obligation bonds sometimes provide an even safer haven. GO bonds enable the state or municipality to levy additional taxes to repay the bonded indebtedness if the issuer cannot. However, as we saw in the case of Detroit, even GOs can crater at the hands of unscrupulous politicians bent on getting themselves reelected rather than placing the interests of their constituents ahead of their own and upholding the laws they were elected to honor. Plus, there was little capacity to pay additional taxes since so much of the Detroit population fled the city long ago.

Solution: Credit enhancement programs
There's a safety net for fixed income investors. These are the so-called credit enhancement programs offered by 21 states and used by their local governments and school districts. The program allows these small municipal bond issuers to bump up their rating to something close to that of their state. Suddenly, these smaller issuers can lower their borrowing costs while

attracting the interest of quality-conscious investors.

Solution: Four types of safety nets

The most common safety nets and credit enhancement programs you'll encounter include:

- State guaranty programs
- State aid intercept/withholding programs
- State appropriation programs
- Fund programs

The Official Statements of each bond issue detail the mechanics of that particular state enhancement program, along with the credit rating.

State Guaranty Programs

Using this program, the state pledges its full faith and credit to stand behind local bonds. Should the local bond issuer fail, the state will use general fund reserves or issue GO bonds, if necessary, to replace the issuer's debt service deficiencies. This program is designed to ensure that no interest or principal payment is ever missed regardless of the financial capability of the bond issuer. Bonds in this gold-plated program are the same as the state's general credit rating. Four states with successful guaranty programs include Michigan, Oregon, Utah, and Washington.

State Aid Intercept/Withholding Programs:
Simply stated, these programs require states
to redirect state aid payments normally paid
to bond issuer city, town or school district to
the bond trustee should the issuer fail to
make its debt service payments. This
intercept of funds automatically kicks in
should the issuer fail to make timely and
complete payment due on their bonds.

The big three rating agencies recognize this
credit enhancement program. That means
Moody's, S&P and Fitch are all likely to
raise the credit rating of a municipality or
school district up to their state's rating or
something close to it. Without the credit
enhancement, the small issuer would be on
their own and either not be rated or would
receive the rating their limited resources
deserve.

Many states have intercept programs.
Among them are:

1. Colorado
2. Georgia
3. Massachusetts
4. New Mexico
5. New York
6. Ohio
7. Pennsylvania
8. Indiana
9. Kentucky
10. Mississippi
11. Missouri
12. South Dakota
13. Virginia

Intercept bonds have the benefit of putting
bondholders first in the line of creditors to

get paid with state aid revenues before the issuer can get their hot little hands on them.

Here's how it works in the real world. Say the New Jersey Qualified Bond Program authorizes the state treasurer to intercept state aid due to cities, towns, and school districts. If the local bond issuer fails to allocate enough money to make bond payments, the state grabs funds that it would normally pay to the issuing entity and routs them to the bond trustee for payment to the bondholders.

Not only does this program improve the bond rating of these small issuers, it lowers the interest they have to pay because the bonds carry less risk of default. Further, it allows these small issuers access to a broader investor market due to their improved rating.

There is a caveat: Make sure the state is creditworthy and can step in if needed. We've illustrated the financial problems of Illinois. They don't have an intercept program. If they did, it wouldn't provide much in the way of credit enhancement because their own credit rating is so dismally low.

State Appropriation Programs
State Appropriation Programs require payment of state funds to make whole any shortfall in debt service by participating school districts. We don't see this quite as good a safety net as the intercept programs. Especially since some programs have

standing appropriations, while others require annual appropriation renewal by their legislatures. So you might own a bond in the program whose annual appropriation was not renewed. What then? Your bond is suddenly downgraded and will likely plummet in value.

State Fund Programs
Similar to appropriation programs, State Funds will usually divert money from constitutionally created funds specifically for this purpose to bond trustees. This happens if participating school districts cannot make timely payment on their bonds. Since these funds are not linked to the state, ratings on these programs generally don't carry the corresponding state's rating.

The safety of bonds participating in State Fund Programs depends on the size of the fund and whether state officials can get their hands on the funds to divert to other purposes.

One of our favorite bond safety nets is the **Texas Permanent School Fund**. The state created the fund back in 1854 with a $2 million appropriation by the Texas Legislature. It was specifically earmarked for the benefit of the public schools of Texas. The state was very smart in what they did. The Texas Constitution of 1876 stipulated that certain lands and all proceeds from the sale of these lands should belong to the PSF. Over the years more public land—along with their water and mineral rights—were given to the PSF.

The most recent valuation we've found for the Texas PSF was in January 2015 when the fund had a guarantee capacity of $80 billion. These funds are professionally managed. They are invested in a diversified mix of equities; fixed income; land, minerals and real assets; and alternative investments. Since few municipal bond issuers in the Texas program will fail, the Fund is allowed to guarantee bond issues up to 2.5 times the fund value.

Fitch has rated the Texas PSF Fund as AAA. This superior rating also goes to those municipal bonds guaranteed by the Texas Fund. Truly, this far-reaching program has allowed access to capital markets by Texas school districts that they could never have achieved without it.

Solution: Evaluate the credit enhancement program

There are a few things we always look at when evaluating the safety net created by a credit enhancement program. It takes a little legwork, but it can save your portfolio from a devastating loss. Here are the things we believe every investor should be aware of:

Permanency of the fund
Only Nevada, Texas, and Wyoming operate permanent funds to enhance school debt. They are capitalized with hard assets—real estate, mineral rights, and royalties. If a district defaults and must tap the fund, they must repay the fund.

Payment timing
The strongest programs step in and transfer money for bond payment if the bond trustee doesn't receive the cash needed to cover the upcoming payment from the district within fifteen days *before* it is due. We like that. Weaker programs don't step in and fund until *after* a default has occurred—as in the case of Indiana described below.

Contractual agreement
The stronger programs—such as New York—have an unbreakable contractual pledge to step in and pay bondholders. Weaker programs allow legislators to rewrite intercept laws as they please— possibly to the detriment of bondholders.

State monitoring
New Jersey's Local Finance Board and its Department of Education monitor municipal and school budgets to ensure compliance not only with state laws but also with their debt service obligations. They have sufficient advance warning of an impending default that could trigger the intercept program.

Third party notification of default
We call this the cat in the hen house clause. The strongest programs hire independent third parties to provide state officials with notification of default. The weaker programs delegate this responsibility to the districts themselves. If there's fraud, embezzlement, or simple incompetence, the state will likely never hear of it until it is too late.

Solution: Safety nets are not perfect
Even intercept bonds carry a degree of risk. Take the Indiana school district of Munster,

for example. Munster boasts some of the highest student test scores in the state. Their bonds are part of the state's intercept program. No problem, many investors said. Yes and no. In January 2015 Munster defaulted on payment of two of its bonds due to a $2.2 million revenue shortfall.

The event of default lasted only three days before school district officials were able to accumulate the needed funds and make the payment. The state treasurer never needed to step in to make the payment for the district. Actually, the district never even spoke with the state about the default.

However, this event brings up an important caution. Just because a bond is backstopped by a safety net such as an intercept program, doesn't mean investors can ignore current events shaping their bond's future. In Munster's case, the handwriting was on the wall for anyone interested enough to look— as we were. Indiana has made some drastic cuts to school district funding and changed the funding formula on which they base district funding. So the money these school districts counted on to be there when their bonds were issued, suddenly wasn't available.

When such a cash shortfall happens to any municipal issuer, they must cut spending immediately. Easy to say. But in the real world it doesn't work that way. Spending cuts and layoffs of valued employees take time. For Munster, they laid off 50 non-teacher employees out of 400. There has been no word on the amount of further spending cuts, if any.

Don't trust the ratings
Apparently, Standard & Poor's wasn't satisfied either. They put Munster's bonds on negative credit watch. However, S&P did not downgrade Munster from its BBB rating. We fail to understand how they affirmed an investment grade rating in the face of an event of default. S&P's negative credit watch note says there's a one-in-two likelihood of them downgrading the bonds in the near future. At least that's something.

S&P's failure to immediately downgrade these bonds speaks volumes about the trust investors should have in the raw ratings. Not much. Always look behind the ratings and see what is happening with the bond issuer. In Munster's case, a little research would have unearthed a potential can of worms that might have changed investor's minds.

We took our own advice and did some more research based on the cockroach theory— there's never just one. We discovered $8 million of taxable pension bonds placed by the Munster school district among its $97 million of outstanding debt and lease obligations. How safe are these pension bonds? Questionable, in our opinion. If a new client came to Envision Capital owning these bonds, we would sell them immediately.

Chapter 4: Weak States Cannot Afford To Bail Out Their Cities

States suffering economic ills themselves will have a difficult time bailing out their cities when they run into difficulty. Indeed, the idea that a state can somehow afford things for its citizens that they cannot afford for themselves is absurd.

Headlining recent news is the decline and volatility in oil prices. Several states— Texas, Alaska, Louisiana, New Mexico, Oklahoma, and North Dakota—are oil states. A substantial part of their revenue is linked in some way to the price of oil.

Oklahoma is a case in point. Its budget shortfall doubled to $611 million for the coming year. The state has falling revenues from oil and rising layoffs. Still, it has $535 million in its unallocated rainy day fund. Are their bonds in trouble? Perhaps, we say. Certainly, with the drop in oil prices and a $249 million drop in income tax collections projected for 2016, we would watch any Oklahoma bonds or bonds with the state's backing.

Even with declining oil prices and a dependency on maintaining oil prices, Oklahoma is in much better shape than Alaska. Oklahoma receives just four percent of its general revenues from oil production taxes. Alaska gets 90 percent of its general revenues from oil production taxes. By contrast, Louisiana is another oil dependent state. But they get just 16 percent of their general revenues from oil production taxes. They have revised downward their revenue projections for 2015 through 2016 and now face a budget gap of $1.6 billion for fiscal 2016.

Damage: Help us out here, Governor
How will municipalities fare when they ask their governors for assistance and the answer is to pound sand? We fear the solution these states and municipalities ultimately come up with will go against the bondholders.

This occurred in Detroit's bankruptcy. There, the pensions—benefiting some voters and supported by the unions that sway large blocks of voters—received an extraordinary deal. Detroit's General Obligation bondholders received just 74 cents on the dollar in the bankruptcy settlement. The Limited GO bondholders got even less—34 cents on the dollar.

Bondholders do not vote—at least not usually in large numbers in the jurisdiction where the bonds were issued. Politics and finance have merged. That seems to be the reality at work. The side with the strongest voting block wins. Bondholders have no voting block—just the bond indenture and the law—on their side. Not enough anymore.

Our fear is that Detroit's bankruptcy success in abusing its bondholders to help solve its financial problems will become the standard by which other municipalities facing bankruptcy will operate. We're already seeing the beginnings of that in Atlantic City with the same bankruptcy advisor who engineered the Detroit bankruptcy that proved so disastrous for bondholders.

Damage: Fund managers protect their wallet

The municipal bond fund managers will publicly disagree. They tell the financial media that there's no problem with owning municipal bonds in these weakened states and the bonds are money good. Look behind those comments and follow the money. These questionable bonds carry a higher yield for good reason—they're risky. This lures yield-starved investors into their funds which ramps up their fees as the yield hogs stampede in. These bonds may ultimately prove not to be money good, but they do put money in the pockets of the municipal bond fund managers.

Damage: The Government will bail out the cities

We've heard this argument before from investors rationalizing their risky investment in a municipal bond issued by a weak municipality in a weak state. Their rationale seems to be that the federal government will not let our cities fail.

We disagree. The city of Detroit failed and was not bailed out by the federal government. How would such a bailout work? The Fed would have to step in and buy the outstanding municipal bonds issued by the failed city. Then the Fed would arrange some sort of restructure that fit the city's ability to pay.

However, the Fed only has legal authority to buy muni debt with maturities of six months or less. And such bonds must be directly backed by tax or other assured revenue. Bonds like this make up less than two percent of the overall market. The Dodd-Frank financial-regulation law further tied the Fed's hands, by barring the Fed from lending to insolvent borrowers or arranging bailouts of individual borrowers."

That's not to say such a bailout of a major city can't happen. Chicago is one city that worries us. The windy city has $8.3 billion in General Obligation debt outstanding. Moody's rates these bonds the lowest among the 90 biggest cities at Baa2 with a negative outlook. Two more ratings downgrades and Chicago bonds turn into junk bonds. But wait. There's more bad news. Chicago has $20 billion in unfunded pension liabilities.

It gets even worse. Chicago dabbled in interest rate swaps on their debt. With Moody's rating downgrade the city may have to pay $400 million to unwind some of these swaps that stipulate a minimum credit rating. Should there be further rating downgrades, Chicago may be forced to unwind even more of their swaps.

Our conclusion is to stay out of all Illinois and Chicago bonds unless they have some sort of credible safety net behind them.

* * *

Chapter 5: Corporate Bonds

Corporate bonds most definitely have a place in every fixed income portfolio. Corporate bonds carry the rating of their issuing corporation, based on credit history and ability to repay obligations. These are usually (but not always) companies whose stock is also held by the public. As such they are subject to the rules and regulations of the SEC. Generally, the SEC deals with publicly held corporations in a swifter and stricter manner than they do municipalities. This is the kind of oversight we expect from those charged with monitoring our securities.

Corporates also afford investors diversity in their holdings. All types of corporations issue bonds. They come from every industry and are located all around the country. They have every grade of rating to choose from. If diversification is one of your investment goals, corporates must be on your shopping list.

The market for corporate bonds is robust. As long as you invest in an issue at least $300 million in size, chances are you won't have a problem selling the bonds when you wish at the fair market value. Investors get into trouble when they buy into a corporate bond issue that has a very small float—less than $300 million. At that point, often the pool of investors is quite small. There isn't a large enough market to fairly price bonds traded. Indeed, such small issue bonds may trade only rarely.

Corporates are not without their problems for individual investors. We've come up with several of which we want you to be aware.

Now is the era of M&A

Regardless of the company's name as they announce their take over of another corporation, shareholders may be overjoyed. Not so much for the bondholders—on either side of the transaction. The poor bondholders are likely destined for heavily leveraged balance sheets. Not a good thing. The more debt glommed onto a balance sheet, the lower the critical metrics defining the safety of the underlying bonds. The all-important debt coverage ratio is among them. The higher the debt, the lower this critical ratio. If it falls low enough, the bonds may be downgraded.

If the deal was done by a private equity group, the more debt the better, so far as they're concerned. With the bond proceeds the private equity firms sometimes declare themselves a humongous dividend and recoup their investment almost immediately. That's one way they get their money out of the deal.

Solution: Change of control
How would you feel if you awoke one morning to see that your A rated corporate bond had turned to junk overnight? That's what can happen if your bond issuer was suddenly taken over in a leveraged transaction. Suddenly your issuer is saddled with mountains of bond debt to pay for the

purchase. The balance sheet sinks below the waterline and is immediately downgraded.

But wait. There's a way to protect yourself. Before you ever buy a corporate bond ask your broker if there's a *change of control provision*. This clause in the bond indenture allows you to sell back your bond to the issuer usually at a price of 101 ($1010 per bond) in the event of a merger or corporate takeover. Without this all-important change of control provision, you have no protection from acquisition hounds. They will load your company with debt and pocket the cash, sending the value of your bond into a tailspin.

Here's a history lesson on what can happen without a COC provision. Remember when the private equity firm Apollo acquired Harrah's back in 2006? Before the acquisition Harrah's bonds were rated BBB-. They were on their way to being upgraded. But…with announcement of Apollo's acquisition the bonds were slammed down ten points in the first trade of the day. That's a dip in value of $100 per bond.

Now here's what happens when there is a COC provision to save bondholders. A few years ago the Blackstone Group announced its purchase of Equity Office Properties. There was a COC provision. No problem for the bondholders. They simply sold back their bonds to the issuer at the stipulated price of 101. If they had purchased these bonds at any kind of a discount, they were happy with their profit. Today, large institutional bond buyers demand change of control protection. So should you.

Solution: Post acquisition—sell or keep
Investors whose bonds are not nuked immediately after announcement that their company has been acquired have a decision to make. Should they sell anyway or hang on to their bonds? Coming up with the right answers requires some thought.

Why was the company acquired in the first place? Almost always just two reasons offer motivation for an acquisition:

1. There's a strategic gap the company can fill

2. The acquisition aids the company in entering a new market

Ask yourself if your company actually can help its new parent accomplish these two goals. If not, then sell.

Over half of all acquisitions fail. If you choose to hang onto your bonds you don't want to be among the failures. The most common reasons that acquisitions crater revolve around overly high valuations, misunderstood value drivers by the parent and a mismatch of corporate cultures. If you see any (or all) of these problems, then sell.

Lastly, acquisitions spawn employee turnover. This can be good in terms of eliminating redundant positions and replacing dead wood. However, sometimes the most talented people end up leaving. If you see announcements of the most talented people who are responsible for your company's success leaving, then sell.

At Envision Capital we're constantly on the lookout for potential acquisitions of our issuers. When they happen, we act decisively and swiftly. Here's an excerpt from an email we sent clients explaining our actions related to the acquisition of Family Dollar Corp. by Dollar Tree:

You recently received or will receive a confirmation of the sale of your Family Dollar corporate bonds. There was a corporate tug-of-war over buying the Family Dollar company between Dollar General and Dollar Tree: Dollar Tree was the winner.

Although our bonds had a Change of Control Provision at 101 ($1010 per bond) we didn't want to wait considering bonds in the secondary market were trading over 105 ($1050 per bond). Also, this acquisition will require Dollar Tree to issue much more debt thereby turning our once investment grade bonds into junk. This is an $8.8 billion merger so there will be more debt galore.

Make sure that you understand the logic behind such trades by your money manager. If you don't, then ask them. If you can't reach them or they don't have a plausible answer, change money managers.

Solution: Predict the takeover

You may be worried that your bond issuer is about to be taken over. With that transaction comes the debt and the general weakening of your company's balance sheet.

There are ways to predict the possibility of a takeover. First, look at the atmosphere of confidence in your issuer's industry. M&A usually ramps up when CEOs have confidence in the economy, their industry, and their markets. They decline without that confidence—such as could happen in the face of Middle East instability, terrorist acts, or a protracted union strike that affects their ability to get critical supplies.

If you believe there's CEO confidence in your industry, then drill just a little deeper into your analysis. Look at the M&A activity in your industry. Is it increasing? Why? For example, healthcare is an active industry for M&A. That's due in part to Obamacare and its impact on the industry. Healthcare competitors see Obamacare as a disruptive influence in a once orderly industry. They want to reposition themselves to either defend their market share or increase it. That means M&A activity.

The telecom industry is also on the forefront of M&A but for a different reason. As we write this, Comcast is looking to acquire Time/Warner Cable for $69.8 billion including liabilities. AT&T is buying DirecTV for $48.5 billion. Why? To increase their share of home video subscribers. AT&T had to make their acquisition to keep up with Comcast in this highly competitive industry.

The pharmaceutical industry is another candidate for M&A. Competitors need to consolidate and cut costs until revenues ramp back up to earlier levels.

The force of activists
There are a number of well-known shareholder activists that bond investors keep a close watch on. Carl Icahn is certainly one of them. If one of these activists holds a stock position in your issuer and they begin their shareholder value dance, an acquisition is a definite possibility. That is how Forest Labs—maker of medications for everything from dementia to irritable bowel syndrome—accepted the takeover deal proposed by Actavis. Icahn was instrumental in making Forest see the light.

Predicting a takeover of your company should include these three things:

1. CEO confidence

2. Disruptions in your issuer's market that require a response by competitors

3. Reaction to the acquisition of one competitor on the part of another

If you believe your issuer has a substantial likelihood of being acquired and it will adversely affect your bond value, then sell ahead of the transaction.

Finally, check to see that your bonds have a Change Of Control provision. If they do, then you are in good shape in the event of an unexpected acquisition. **There's a caution here.** Not all bond issues of a company have the same COC protection. Some issues from the same company will; some won't. You must read the bond indenture *of your specific bond* to find out if it exists and what it says.

* * *

Chapter 6: Tendering Bonds

If you've been a bond investor for some time, chances are you've come across a bond tender offer. Depending on what you decide, your bond portfolio could be significantly affected.

Bond tender offers come when the issuer wishes to retire all or a portion of a bond issue. Essentially, the bond issuer is repurchasing its debt. Tender offers usually state a predetermined number of bonds, the price being offered, and the deadline date for tendering the bonds. Most tender offers are for bonds that don't have a near call date.

The benefit to the issuer by making a tender offer is restructuring their cost of capital to something less than what it was before. If interest rates have come down significantly since your bonds were issued, the company will conduct a new bond offering at a lower coupon rate. It then uses the proceeds to fund a buy-back and retirement of the older, high coupon bonds. That's how they effectively lower their cost of capital.

Tender offers don't always replace one high coupon bond issue with a lower one. Sometimes a highly leveraged company that is flush with unallocated cash will use some of it to simply retire older high coupon bonds without replacing them with a new issue. This transaction lowers both their cost of capital as well as their debt/equity ratio.

Damage: Reduced liquidity
When we speak of liquidity in the bond market, we're talking about the float of a bond issue. This is simply the number of bonds out on the market. There must be sufficient bonds, held by a sufficient number of investors to create an orderly market. We believe a bond issue of at least $300 million provides sufficient liquidity.

However, what happens if a bond tender offer comes from the issuing company and it's only for a portion of an issue? Or it may be for the entire issue, but not all the bondholders tender their bonds. Either way, you as the bondholder have a critical decision to make.

You can tender your bonds and eliminate the risk of not having sufficient liquidity in the bond issue to sell when you want to. Or you can elect not to tender your bonds. Your decision not to tender your bonds revolves around having to replace them with lower yielding bonds. Your income stream will decline if you tender.

Here's the risk you run. You've resigned yourself to taking the hit to your fixed income stream. So you decide to tender your bonds. But fewer of your fellow bondholders tendered their bonds. In this case there's still sufficient float out there to maintain an orderly market and you could sell anytime you wish. You took a hit to your income that was unnecessary. Idiot, you tell yourself.

The risk of *refusing* to tender your bonds also revolves around liquidity. If you don't tender your bonds, but most every other bondholder does, there may not be sufficient liquidity for you to sell the bonds when you want to at a fair market value. You'll have to hold them until maturity. In a bond market where yields are rising, this will diminish the value of your bond portfolio. Idiot, you tell yourself again. But this time it comes from being greedy for those few basis points you insisted on keeping. You may have lost significantly more than that in the reduction to principal you had no choice in taking as you sold into a falling, illiquid market.

Investor's objective of tendering bonds
Tendering bonds can be a game of guessing what the other bondholders will do. If you tender you hope that almost all of the other bondholders will also tender. This says that the bonds have run their course. Because so much of the issue was tendered there just isn't sufficient liquidity remaining to warrant taking the risk that you can sell the bonds at the tender price should they decline in value.

For example, Wynn Las Vegas tendered for $1.33 billion in bonds due in 2020. The next call date was August 15, 2015. Envision Capital held these bonds in its client's individually managed portfolios. We tendered. Rightly so. Now just $80 million of these bonds remain on the market, owned by those few geniuses who decided not to tender. The bonds still occasionally trade. However, we don't believe there is sufficient liquidity and enough individual bondholders to create a market large enough to provide a fair value for those diehards to sell when they wish.

* * *

Chapter 7: Financial Engineering

There are many types of financial engineering plays being done in the market now. In every case, the intent seems to trade real business innovation and enhanced profitability for cosmetic changes that make the company *appear* like something it is not. Senior management hopes the company's stock will rise as a result. Not to be cynical, but it is these same chief executive's whose compensation package is tied to stock price.

The frequency of financial engineering plays increases as bull markets wind out. Gone are the truly innovative strategies that raise a company's profitability and cash flow, thereby increasing their stock price. The end of bull markets utilizes the window dressing that financial engineering creates to raise stock prices.

Five types of financial engineering
Any time a company adds more debt without an incremental improvement in profitability and free cash flow, bonds suffer. To us bondholders, this additional debt produced nothing of value to the company. The two most common types of financial engineering that adversely affects bondholders is the leveraged stock buyback and dividend payments. Both often paid for from the proceeds of a bond issue. Rather than invest the bond proceeds in the business, the CEO chooses to buy the company's stock back. This only serves to

artificially raise the stock price as its float dwindles. More on this later.

The second kind of financial engineering we see is an upswing in mergers and acquisitions. We call this, *restless capital syndrome.* As the market cycle matures, CEOs need to appear that they're doing something. Anything. So buying a company using debt as the currency of choice seems to be the accepted way for the CEO to look busy.

The third type of engineering we see appears within the ranks of the private equity firms. They cannot find the golden acorn in fresh and innovative companies to invest in and grow. Or they're unwilling to wait out the gestation period. Instead, they begin trading their portfolio companies among themselves. Usually these trades occur when a portfolio company at one private equity firm is valued more highly by another, competing firm. Perhaps there's some sort of strategic synergy with one of their portfolio companies. The first company needs to show some sort of return on its investment for the company. So they sell it.

The fourth financial engineering play we see are the so-called tax inversion mergers. The strategy here is to move the company's corporate headquarters beyond the reach of US taxing authorities. It's the same company, now minus the tax liability at the exceedingly high US tax rates. Sometimes this strategy raises the stock price. However, there's a cost—several costs, actually. They must build a new home office in the tax haven country and move the key employees there. Then, they'll likely spend tens of millions on consultants and advisors both on the tax issues and the move. Finally, there's the soft cost of losing public relations points with suppliers, consumers and customers.

The fifth type of financial engineering attempts to convert the company to an asset class *that seems* to be in favor at the moment. As we write this booklet, real estate is currently in favor. Many companies are trying to qualify themselves under US tax laws as REITs. Their hope is that investors will suddenly view them as a yield producing real estate asset. One example is Corrections Corp. of America—the private prison operator. Suddenly they're out of the human warehousing business and into the rising real estate industry.

There's also the outdoor advertising industry. Both CBS Outdoor Corp and Lamar Advertising Co. converted themselves into REITs. Even the computer server farm, Equinix Corp., managed to fulfill the requirements of becoming a REIT.

In each of these cases, the company's share prices rose even though the business remained fundamentally unchanged.

Moving money from one pocket to another Investor activists like Carl Ichan are equity players. Their mission is to raise the stock price any way they can and as quickly as they can. They want the money. The CEOs response to this is to buy back the company's stock or declare a special dividend paid for using the proceeds from a new bond issue. Indeed, the cash from companies buying back their own stock exceeds fresh cash coming into US equities by a margin of six to one.

During 2014 there was $550 billion in corporate stock buybacks. That's $46 billion per month. During that year, individual investors selling a stock on US exchanges quite often were selling it back to the issuing companies.

If you're a shareholder in these companies active in buybacks, you likely made money. The S&P Buyback Index tracks the stock price of the 100 companies with the highest stock repurchase ratio.

Problem is this type of financial engineering only increases the *optics* of the company's profitability. When the analysts go to compute earnings per share, they see a fewer number of shares to use as their divisor. Consequently, their EPS calculations *appear* to show a significant improvement.

However, nothing good has occurred at the company. Earnings before tax have not gone up. Free cash flow from operations is not any better than it previously was. The company is still exactly the same as it was. So the CEO has simply pulled money out of the bondholder's pockets in the form of a more highly leveraged balance sheet. They gave that money to shareholders in the form of higher share prices or a special dividend. The shareholders—especially the activists— are happy. They can now sell their shares at a significant profit and move on to their next conquest. The bondholders are left holding the bag.

Soaring debt levels

Due mostly to funding stock buybacks and dividends, the debt of US corporations is soaring. Since the crash of 2008, corporate debt has increased by a whopping *$2 trillion.* Note the sudden increase in 2008 as it takes off in the graph below.

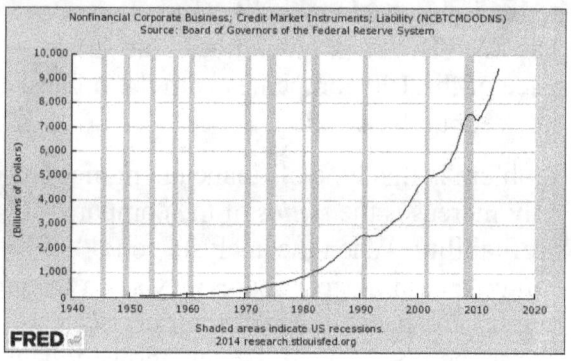

Now we see that these companies are buying back their own shares at the upper reaches of their historical highs. Essentially, these executives are buying high and selling low. Historically, peaks in share buybacks have foretold major market tops.

Why are the CEOs doing this? Wouldn't it have been better to buy these same shares back in 2009 or 2010 when they were 50 percent of their current high prices? The answer has to do with how chief executive compensation is structured. It's based on the stock price.

The danger we see with all of this debt at never-before-seen levels is two-fold. First, interest rates will rise sometime in the future. When they do, these same high-flying companies will have a hard time repaying these debts. Second, the economy will slow at some time in the future. Since so many of these companies don't have the ability to ever fully repay this debt, they've placed themselves in the position of *having* to roll it over in what we see as possibly future adverse conditions.

The following chart published by the ETFGuide shows quite well the huge divergence between new corporate debt and the cash needed to repay it:

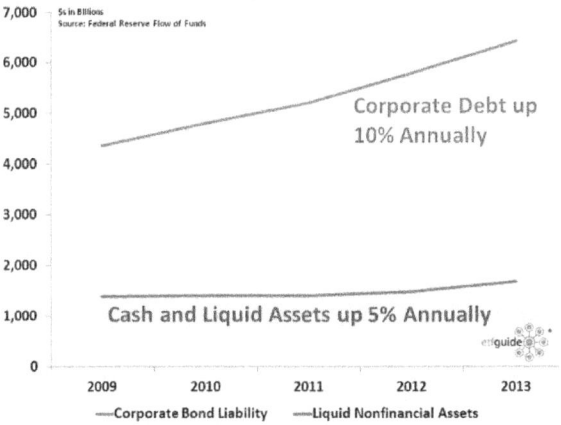

As bond investors, we're skeptical of the financial media. They talk about the ever-improving corporate balance sheets. We don't see it. Debt has increased by $2 trillion while liquid assets have only risen by $0.3 trillion. In our view, that's a shaky inverted

pyramid built on the need to give
shareholders a shortsighted and temporary
pop to their stock price.

* * *

Chapter 8: The Bondholder's Worst Nightmare

Bondholders actually have many potential nightmares. However, the one we count at the top of the list is restatement. This term refers to the financial statements and it's not good news. When a company announces that it must restate its financial results, it means someone blew it—usually unintentionally, but sometimes not.

The Sarbanes-Oxley Act of 2002, section 302, "Corporate Responsibility for Financial Reports," requires the CEO and CFO of publicly traded companies to certify their company's financial statements and disclosures that "they fairly present, in all material respects, the operations and financial condition of the company."

Understand that this is nothing new. For decades CEOs and CFOs have been providing the same assurances to their auditors in the auditor's Management Representation Letter. It simply states that management made certain representations to the auditor, both oral and written, in response to specific inquiries or through the financial statements. These representations are part of the evidential matter that independent auditors collect to support their overall opinion of the financials. Indeed, this rep letter is often attached as a Management's Responsibility for Financial Reporting Letter in the corporation's annual report.

In today's regulatory environment, this attestation to the accuracy of the company's financial statements also appears—usually at the end—of the Form 10-k and annual report of publicly held companies. The CEO and the CFO sign these assertions that the financial statements are accurate. Here's what the CEO's certification for Apple looks like in its 10-k report:

I, Timothy D. Cook, certify, as of the date hereof, pursuant to 18 U.S.C. Section 1350, as adopted pursuant to Section 906 of the Sarbanes-Oxley Act of 2002, that the Annual Report of Apple Inc. on Form 10-K for the fiscal year ended September 27, 2014 fully complies with the requirements of Section 13(a) or 15(d) of the Securities Exchange Act of 1934 and that information contained in such Form 10-K fairly presents in all material respects the financial condition and results of operations of Apple Inc. at the dates and for the periods indicated.

Date: October 27, 2014

Timothy D. Cook

Timothy D. Cook

Chief Executive Officer

Damage: Restatement of financials
Putting embarrassment aside—for the CEO, CFO and auditors—a company that must restate its financials now has a credibility

problem with its investors. They have just told the world that the numbers they published and swore were correct, are not. For we bondholders that is like a knife through the heart. We base our buy, sell, and hold decisions on the financial statements as well as interim guidance from management. If the information they provided and that we acted on is now wrong, we have a big problem. The decisions we made regarding the company's bonds may also not be what we would have done had we known the correct numbers. For bondholders, restatements can be very costly.

For example, a restatement could reduce the amount of cash reserves by a material amount. If it's large enough, the financial ratios on which the rating agencies base their judgment may be much lower. Worst case, the rating agencies lower the company's rating. In the very worst case the lowered rating plunges the company below investment grade. The institutional bondholders of this issue—with an exclusive mandate for investment grade—have no choice but to sell. Suddenly, there's a massive flood of the company's bonds in the market—all sellers and no buyers. The bond price plunges. All because the company couldn't (or wouldn't) get its numbers right.

The most troublesome restatements are those that cause a company's sales, income, liquidity, or financial position to change from what was previously reported. Not every restatement does this. Still, it's better to get the numbers right the first time. Credibility in the financial arena counts.

Damage: The costs of restatement
Whether a restatement involves an annual
report, a quarterly report, or even guidance
from the CEO or CFO, there will be huge
costs involved. First, the company will
launch an investigation—usually headed by
the audit committee of the board of
directors—of the company's accounting
practices and systems of internal accounting
controls.

Heads will likely roll. Often the CFO is
replaced along with the audit firm. New
employees are hired to be sure the problem
never happens again.

The most potentially damaging cost of
restatement is the drop in stock and bond
values. These can be in the billions. Hertz
restated its earnings guidance for 2014. The
stock plunged 10 percent immediately.
Coincidentally, investor/activist Carl Icahn
purchased an 8.5 percent stake in Hertz.
This interest by Icahn caused the stock to
rally. Investors wondered what Icahn knew
that either they didn't know or that the
company hadn't yet disclosed.

Hard costs associated with restatements
revolve around legal, accounting and
consulting fees. When Tech Data restated its
2012 financial statements in 2013 it
estimated direct associated costs were over
$50 million. Along with the outside
professionals it hired to fix the financial
statements, its audit committee investigated
the company's accounting procedures. They
implemented a slew of supplemental review

procedures and practices to ensure the problem would not be repeated. The restatement expenses flowed into 2015, largely related to the supplemental procedures and practices that are ongoing.

Along with Hertz and Tech Data many other companies have restated their financial results. Among them are Waste Management, Xerox, Rite Aid, Safety-Kleen, and Thomas & Betts.

Solution: Decide and act immediately
For individual investors there's not much you can do about the affect restatements have on your portfolio. It's more a matter of; *you don't know what you don't know.* Still, if you make your decisions and act immediately on hearing news of a restatement, you might lessen the blow.

Sometimes, the market is slow to react. As an individual investor you have no investment committee to convene for permission to pull the trigger on a bond that is restating its financials to the downside. If you act quickly, you can sometimes execute a sale somewhere at or near a fair market price before it begins its downward tumble.

There's a flip side to this independence. Often having a collaborative team can help prevent an unnecessary sale of a bond whose restatement turns out to be a non-event. This happened with Hertz. We thought the bonds were going to be nuked on disclosure of the restatement. That turned out not to be the case. Largely due to Carl Icahn's involvement. There was no reason to sell.

Solution: Accounting and the audit firms
The "Global Six" public accounting firms
command about 89 percent of the market for
certified audits. They are Grant Thornton,
E&Y, PWC, KPMG, Deloitte & Toche, and
BDO. The business model for each of these
global accounting firms is one that is
opposed to investor's interests.

Essentially, during an audit these firms
throw the most junior people who cost the
firm the least amount of money into the
audit. The objective is to complete the audit
within the specified time and at the specified
budget. No time is allocated for problems
discovered. These things all preserve the
audit firm's profit margin on the
engagement.

Of course there are more senior people
involved in these audits at various stages.
However, their function is to ensure the
schedule and budgets are met and to render a
clean opinion when done. If they push back
too hard at the client on accounting issues
that affect revenue, earnings and cash flow,
they are likely to lose the client to a
competitor firm. Few partners have the
fortitude to stand up to a client whose fees
represent millions in revenue to their firm.
Things slide, along with professional
judgment.

Financial statements are issued with the
appropriate certifications. The vast majority
of them do indeed fairly represent the
financial condition of the company.
However, sometimes they don't. When that

happens, fingers begin pointing and a restatement occurs.

Solution: Watch for auditors resigning the engagement

If you see your issuer's audit firm replaced and don't agree with the reasons given, dig a little deeper. There may indeed be a problem. Earnings can be artificially inflated using accounting techniques such as accruals. They can overstate revenues before the sale is closed. They can count money that is expected but has not yet actually been paid and received. Accounts receivable might be based on orders for future delivery, ignoring the possibility of cancellation. Sales can be exaggerated by easing credit policies without accruing for the inevitable rise in bad debt expenses. Inventories might deliberately build toward yearend to bump up production figures without accounting for the discount of these excess goods later to dispose of them.

Any of these things are a judgment call by management and the auditors. Sometimes the auditor has such a disagreement with company management on accounting policy or audit procedures that they find it necessary to resign their engagement. They don't want to have their reputation sullied by a failed audit. If you find that to be the case, there is a definite problem with the issuer and you need to sell.

* * *

Chapter 9: Management

A company's management team is only human. They are subject to the same frailties and failures as are all of us. We bondholders count management as a potential risk to our investment. A management that has performed acceptably year after year can become ineffective and destructive. This doesn't usually happen suddenly. Over time management's adverse actions may come to light by astute auditors or employees. Then the company discloses a pattern of incompetence and bad decisions spanning many years but kept under wraps by employees afraid for their own longevity.

When that happens, look for a game of musical chairs in the C-suite. The CEO may be terminated. The CFO may go instead. Or they both may be fired. Any sudden change in the C-suite spells instability in the company—at least for a while. That's a risk for bondholders. We like stability in our cash flow, revenues, capital expenditures and in our management team. When things change without a good explanation, it may be time to sell.

Likewise, management may simply underperform. If competitors are doing well with rising cash reserves and improving debt ratios but your company fails to show the same results, the management team may not be up to the task. The company and it stakeholders are better off without current management's lack of talent. You probably cannot do anything to help management. But you can vote your displeasure by selling their bonds.

Damage: Signs of an incompetent CEO
As a bond investor, you want assurance that the headman, or woman, knows what they're doing. There are some signs that the CEO should be replaced. Here are just a few:

1. **Lack of vision**: They have no idea where they want to take the company. Such a CEO is a follower. The competition will eat your company alive.

2. **Failure to execute**: Even if a CEO has a clearly defined vision of where the company needs to go, the toolbox is still only half full. They must execute and implement their strategy. This requires a clear communicator who makes decisions. The CEO must be an excellent manager and be willing to delegate responsibility and authority. They need to hire the right people, and then get out of their way. If an issuer's CEO cannot execute, sell the bonds.

3. **Adopt to the changing marketplace**: CEOs face new challenges every day. Some come from competitors. Some come from legislators, regulators, and law makers. Some come from suppliers. And some come from customers threatening to take their business elsewhere. CEOs who can't make a decision or consistently make the

wrong decisions are apt to run the company aground. They'll lay the blame somewhere else—anywhere—but themselves. Then they leave with a gold-plated severance package. The bondholders are—once again—left holding the bag. If you see your bond issuer in this dilemma, sell.

4. **They stay in the ivory tower**: Charismatic, competent CEOs are a rare breed. There's no job requirement that the CEO be hugely outgoing, though some are. But they do need to be honest. The best CEOs get out of their offices and act as the face of the company. They meet the press, customers, investors, and bankers. They're not afraid of the tough questions. Indeed, they want to get out there and promote their ideas and ask for feedback. Competent CEOs don't need talking points and notes for interviews. They don't have handlers and lawyers vetting their speeches. If your issuer has a CEO who runs from the public, the media and investors, find out why. Listen to what they have to say, if anything. If you don't agree with them, then sell your bonds.

5. **They're known to the company**: Everyone in the company—from the people on the production line, to the

department heads and everyone in between—know the CEO. They see him or her frequently. They've probably had a conversation or two. They know his or her sense of humor and most importantly they know the CEO's vision, mission and strategy for success. If your issuer has a CEO who is the opposite of this—is largely anonymous—that is not the sign of a true leader. Sell your bonds.

Damage: Overpaid CEOs
We've wondered for a while now how a CEO who is paid tens of millions of dollars a year or more can justify that expense. Who is actually worth that much money? A recent study conducted at the University of Utah by the David Eccles School of Business wondered the same thing. Their conclusion was that the higher a CEO's pay, the worse the performance of their company. Indeed, companies headed by the top 5 percent earning CEOs did 15 percent worse than their peers.

There are many reasons. Most are common sense. The biggest contributor to this apparent disparity between CEO pay and corporate performance revolves around overconfidence. The CEO who is paid so much more than everyone else, carries more weight than everyone else. They may ignore solid advice that is contrary to their own thinking. This overconfidence manifests itself in the acquisitions the company makes. The CEO may overpay for the target company over the objections of just about everyone. These acquisitions rarely garner a positive return.

Another reason has to do with the CEO's tenure in their position. The longer at the helm, the worse their company's performance. This one makes sense. A long standing CEO has more allies on the board. These directors are beholden to the CEO for their lucrative position. They're more likely to go along with the CEO's bad decisions.

Damage: Self-interest
Among the risks of management is the chance that senior executives will place their own interests ahead of the company's and its stakeholders. Recall the scandals of Enron and WorldCom. The management team at both of these companies put their own enrichment ahead of the company's and its stakeholder's welfare. Eventually this greed bankrupted the companies and destroyed the bondholder's investment.

A few years ago there was a battery company called Envia. They raised money from private investors, venture capital, even from the State of California. What California was doing investing taxpayer money in a start-up, we don't know. Anyway, the company produced an engineering breakthrough in the energy density of its lithium-ion battery. The problem is the CEO and co-founder stole the technology from his prior employer. The lawsuit lasted years. Today Envia is no longer in any sort of enviable position.

We view management risk as also applicable to investment managers. Bernie Madoff is the most notorious of these. If you employ an investment manager, pay attention to the way they work. In Madoff's case, the handwriting was on the wall. His sons worked at the firm in senior positions. He led an extraordinarily lavish lifestyle. The firm's independent auditor was a single person with a storefront office in New Jersey. Not what you'd expect for such a large company.

Any one of these things should have raised a question. It didn't because Madoff's *ponzi scheme* provided a lucky few investors with outsized returns. No one wanted to overturn the boat. When reviewing investment managers, the best advice is the smell test. If they don't appear to be conducting business the way you think they should, then move your money elsewhere. Don't wait. Even better to conduct your evaluation before ever hiring them.

Damage: Investor greed
Many investors look at the outsized market results of their issuer's management team and think they know something the rest of the world doesn't. They don't.

In the 2015 world of bond investing, there's not that much difference between average, normal market return and an excess market return. If your portfolio is correctly allocated with no more than 5 percent in any given issuer, then the difference in dollars—even with an outsized return—is pretty small.

However, should the excess market return prove to be a management-induced problem that shakes the company to its core—or even forces it into bankruptcy—the loss of your investment will be catastrophic. It will take years to recoup that loss.

There's a rate for every risk. Bond issuers promising above market returns also carry an above market risk—regardless of what the rating agencies say.

Solution
Owning bonds of a company headed by an incompetent CEO has but one solution. Sell. It may take a while to determine that the CEO is a clueless boob. However, once you've made that determination, don't wait. Sell your bonds and move the money into an issuer with a topflight management team. Waiting and hoping for a change or that the CEO may find religion and become better at their job is silly. There are many corporate bond issuers out there with extraordinarily competent management teams in which to invest. They'll likely prove a much better investment over the long term than the bonds you sold.

* * *

Conclusion

Since the financial crisis, we bond investors have had the wind at our backs—low interest rates, low default rates, high liquidity and Central Bank policies that encourage investment risk. Happily, bond prices have risen.

Stay with this paradigm shift through its end. Attempting to predict the onset of higher interest rates or a massive stock market sell-off never succeeds. Instead, read, make decisions, and stay on top of every bond in your portfolio. It gets even trickier from here.

Best wishes for profitable investing,

Marilyn Cohen & Chris Malburg

* * *

About The Authors

Marilyn Cohen

Marilyn Cohen is one of the country's top bond managers. She began her 35-year financial career as a securities analyst at William O'Neil & Co. She moved into bond brokerage at Cantor Fitzgerald, Inc. then founded Envision Capital Management 20 years ago. As Envision's CEO, Marilyn and her company specializes in managing bond portfolios for individuals.

During this same 20 years Marilyn has written the bond column appearing in

Forbes magazine, and has written three books about investing in bonds.

Marilyn is a popular guest on CNBC, Fox Business News, PBS and each of the major broadcast networks. Contact Marilyn at 800 400-0989 or by email at envision@envisioncap.com.

Chris Malburg

Chris Malburg is a widely published writer. With over 4 million words in print scattered among 25 books and over 100 magazine articles, his work is consumed in most western countries. He writes on the subjects of management, business strategies, and corporate finance. He lives in Southern California with his wife where they are volunteer puppy raisers for Canine Companions for Independence (www.cci.org) and Guide Dogs for the Blind (http://www.guidedogs.com).

* * * *

Connect With Us Online

Marilyn Cohen:

Website: www.Envision@EnvisionCap.com

Chris Malburg:

Website:
www.WritersResourceGroup.com

Twitter:
http://twitter.com/#!/ChrisMalburg

Facebook:
http://facebook.com/chris.malburg

Linkedin:
http://www.linkedin.com/in/chrismalburg

* * * *

A Final Word From The Authors

We hope you enjoyed *The Little Bond eBooklet* and will profit from its lessons. We invite you to enter a review on whatever platform you purchased it. Just log in and give as many stars as you think our effort deserves. Finally, our readers are generous with their emails and tweets. We always make time to answer. If you wish to send us a note, you are welcome to send it to envision@envisioncap.com .

Best wishes,

Marilyn Cohen and Chris Malburg

Other Books By Marilyn Cohen And Chris Malburg

Surviving the Bond Bear Market

Bonds Now!

Bond Bible

About Envision Capital Management, Inc.

Minimum account size: $500,000

Annual fees:

Municipal bonds: .43%

Investment Grade Corporates: .60%

Split rated: .75%

High yield: 1.00%

There are break points in fees depending on account size. Contact us for further details:

Telephone: 800 400-0989

Email: envision@envisioncap.com

Address: 2301 Rosecrans Ave. Suite 4180

El Segundo CA 90245

www.ingramcontent.com/pod-product-compliance
Lightning Source LLC
Chambersburg PA
CBHW070848180526
45168CB00002B/1000